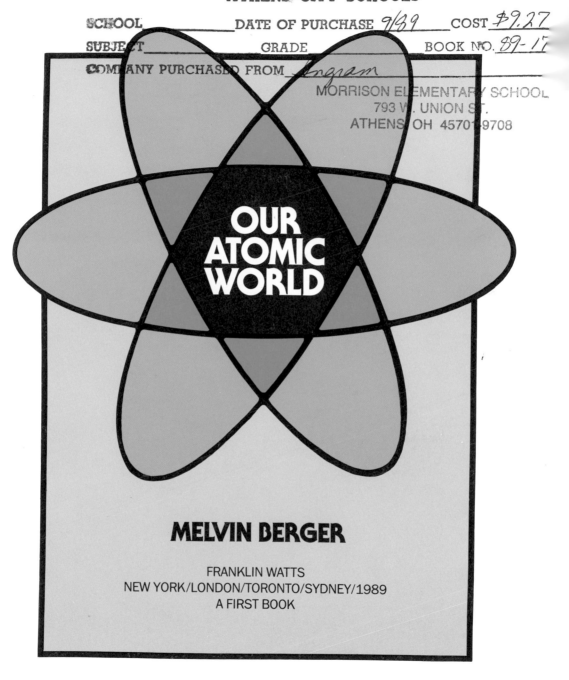

OUR ATOMIC WORLD

MELVIN BERGER

FRANKLIN WATTS
NEW YORK/LONDON/TORONTO/SYDNEY/1989
A FIRST BOOK

Illustrations by Anne Canevari Green

Photographs courtesy of:
Photo Researchers: p. 6 (Claude Noyer), 8, left (Lynn McLaren), 17 (Lawrence Migdale), 19, 36 (Guy Gillette), 38 (below), 39 (David Parker), 41 (Mary Evans Picture Library), 43 (Hank Morgan), 47, below, and 49 (U.S. Department of Energy), 48 (Robert Perron), 53; Peter Arnold: pp. 8, right (Manfred Kage), 11 (David Scharf), 25 (Douglas B. Nelson), 35 (Sybil Shelton), 38, above (Henry Groskinsky), 44 (David J. Cross), 47, center (John Zoiner); New York Public Library Picture Collection: p. 9; NASA: p. 23 (above and center); American Museum of Natural History: p. 23 (below); Los Alamos National Laboratory: p. 47 (above).

Library of Congress Cataloging in Publication Data

Berger, Melvin.
Our atomic world / by Melvin Berger.
p.   cm. — (A First book)
Bibliography: p.
Includes index.
Summary: Introduces basic theories about the nature and behavior of the atom and the field of nuclear physics.
ISBN 0-531-10690-X
1. Atoms—Juvenile literature. 2. Nuclear physics—Juvenile literature. [1. Atoms. 2. Nuclear physics.] I. Title.
II. Series.
QC173.16.B48   1989
539.7—dc19   88-31339   CIP   AC

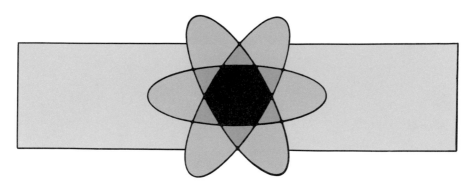

CONTENTS

OUR
ATOMIC
WORLD

Grass and trees, water, the air you breathe—each of these
things is different, yet they are all made up of atoms.

MEET
THE ATOM

Grass and trees.
The food you eat.
The water you drink.
The air you breathe.
You.

Each of these things is different. Yet they are all the same in at least one way. They are all made up of tiny particles called **atoms.** Every single thing in the whole world, in fact, is made up of billions and billions of atoms.

No matter how hard you look, however, you probably won't ever see an atom! Atoms are much too small to be seen with your eyes. Even if you look through the most powerful microscope on earth, you could not see an individual atom.

Atoms are so tiny that there are more of them in a drop of water than there are leaves on all the trees in the world! It takes more than 100 million atoms to make a line 1 inch (2.5 cm) long.

What exactly is an atom?

You can think of an atom as the smallest possible unit of a substance. For example, imagine that you have a gold coin. Cut off a small piece. Then cut that in half. Keep cutting it in half, over and over again. After a while, you have a tiny bit of gold. You keep cutting. Finally, you get the smallest piece of gold possible. This is a single atom of gold.

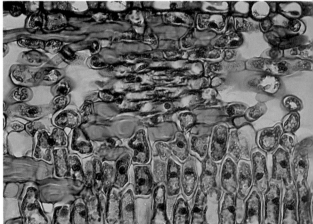

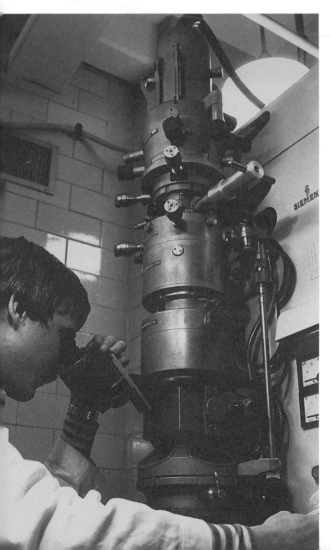

Left: shown is the powerful electron microscope, which lets viewers see matter in greater detail than ever before. However, you still cannot see atoms or parts of atoms. *Above:* we can magnify living things and see detail not possible with the human eye. This photograph shows the cells of the Gnetum leaf. However, we must still guess at what the atoms of matter look like.

The ancient Greek philosopher Democritus

The idea of the atom as the tiniest bit of matter goes back to the ancient Greek philosopher Democritus. Democritus was the first to use the word *atom,* around the year 400 B.C. It comes from the Greek word *atomos,* which means "something that cannot be divided." For more than 2,000 years, scientists believed

that all matter consisted of tiny units called atoms;
that atoms could not be divided;
that all atoms of the same substance were the same;
that atoms of different substances were different; and
that atoms of different substances could join together to form new substances.

Just before the start of the twentieth century, scientists discovered some new things about atoms. They found that atoms *can* be divided. They also learned that inside every atom are even smaller particles. The number and type of particles determine what kind of atom it is. The discovery of the particles inside the atom was one of the most exciting triumphs of modern science.

INSIDE
THE ATOM

Suppose you had super-duper X-ray vision. You could see the smallest things in the universe—things much, *much* tinier than a speck of dust or a grain of sand.

To your eyes, an atom would look somewhat like a ball. But the outside would not appear as solid as a real ball. The surface would be more cloudlike. The shell of an atom has been compared to the blur made by a rapidly spinning fan blade.

This "blur" around the atom is made by tiny particles revolving around the outside at very high speeds. You can see how swirling particles can create a shell that is not really solid. Tie a key at the end of a 3-foot (1-m) length of string. Spin it around in the air as fast as you can. Faster. Faster! Do you see how the spinning key makes a ring in the air?

Some of the particles inside the atom fly around in the same way. They whirl in all directions. Because they move so fast, they blur into a round shell-like covering.

The revolving particles that form a shell around the atom are called **electrons.** The smallest atom, hydrogen, has only one electron revolving around it. Other atoms have more.

Most atoms have more than one electron shell. The largest atom found in nature is uranium. It has six shells of electrons.

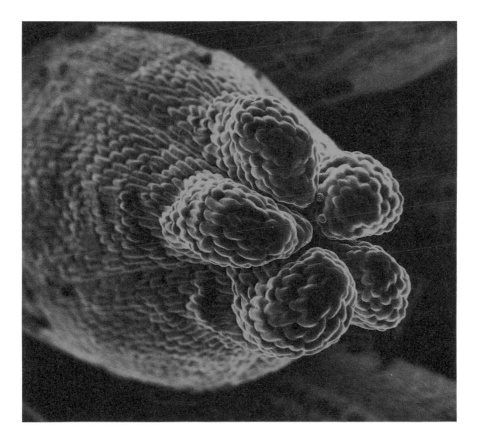

If we all had super-duper X-ray vision, we could see the smaller things in the universe, such as the two pollen grains on this fertilized daisy pistil. Perhaps someday there will be a technology that will let us see the cloudlike surface of the spinning atom.

Each shell can hold only a certain number of electrons:

Shell 1 can have up to 2 electrons;

Shell 2 can have up to 8 electrons;

Shell 3 can have up to 18 electrons;

Shell 4 can have up to 32 electrons;

Shell 5 can have up to 50 electrons; and

Shell 6 can have up to 72 electrons.

Within the shell or shells of whirling electrons there is a lot of empty space. In fact, most of the atom is empty space. At the very center of the atom, though, are more particles. These are packed tightly together and form the **nucleus** of the atom.

Imagine, for a moment, that the electron shell is as big as a blown-up balloon. The nucleus, in that case, would be the size of a grain of sand, right in the balloon's center.

The nucleus is formed of two kinds of particles, **protons** and **neutrons.** Protons and neutrons have about the same mass, which is much more mass than electrons. (Mass is closely related to weight. The mass of an atom, for example, always stays the same. But an atom weighs less on the moon than on earth because of the lower gravity on the moon.) Protons have nearly 2,000 times the mass of electrons.

Protons are different from electrons in another way. Both protons and electrons have electrical charges. But protons have a plus, or positive, electrical charge. Electrons have a minus, or negative, electrical charge.

In electricity, opposite charges attract. It is like the north and south poles of a magnet. They pull toward each other.

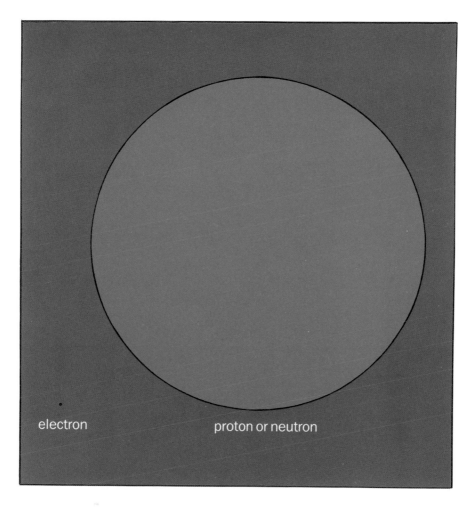

electron   proton or neutron

The mass of an electron is 1/1836 that of a proton or neutron.

The positively charged protons attract the negatively charged electrons. It is this pull, or attraction, that causes the electrons to whirl around the nucleus.

The number of protons in the nucleus is usually the same as the number of electrons. In other words, the protons and

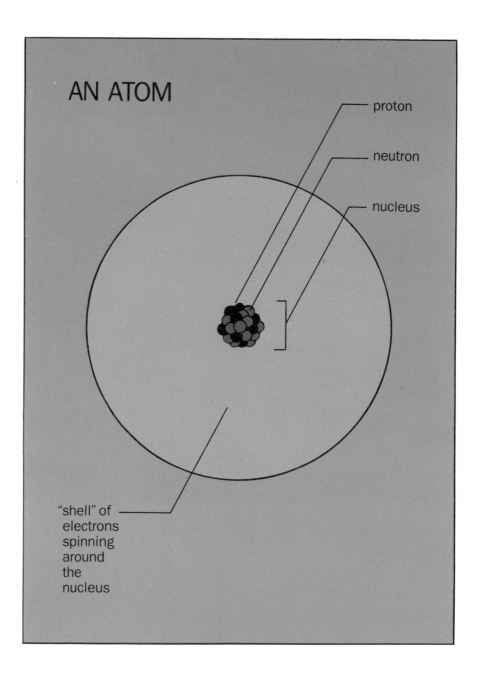

AN ATOM

proton

neutron

nucleus

"shell" of
electrons
spinning
around
the
nucleus

electrons are in balance. The atom has neither a positive nor a negative electrical charge. It is neutral.

For example, an atom of hydrogen has 1 proton and 1 electron. An atom of oxygen has 8 protons and 8 electrons. An atom of uranium has 92 protons and 92 electrons.

Now meet another kind of particle in the nucleus—the neutron. Neutrons have just slightly more mass than protons. The big difference between neutrons and protons is electrical charge. Neutrons are neutral. They have no electrical charge. They are neither positive nor negative.

By now you should have a pretty complete picture of the atom. The outside shell or shells are formed by a cloud or clouds of electrons with a negative charge. Inside is mostly empty space. At the very center is the nucleus. And within the nucleus are found protons, with a positive charge, and neutrons, with no charge.

THE
ELEMENTS

All atoms have a nucleus and a shell of electrons. Yet not all atoms are the same. The difference depends on the number of protons and neutrons they contain. An atom of gold, for example, contains a total of 197 particles in its nucleus—79 protons and 118 neutrons. An atom of silver has 107 particles—47 protons and 60 neutrons.

There are about a hundred different kinds of atoms. A group of identical atoms, all containing the same number of protons, make up an **element.** Although elements always have atoms with the same number of protons, there can be different numbers of neutrons. These are different forms of the element and are discussed below.

You probably know several elements already. Metals such as gold, silver, lead, and iron are elements. So are gases such as oxygen and hydrogen. Carbon, helium, neon, sodium, radium, and chlorine are other elements that may be familiar to you.

PERIODIC TABLE OF ELEMENTS

Key:
Atomic Number — 27
Symbol — Co
Name — Cobalt
Atomic Weight — 58.9332

IA	IIA	IIIB	IVB	VB	VIB	VIIB	VIII	VIII	VIII	IB	IIB	IIIA	IVA	VA	VIA	VIIA	0
1 H Hydrogen 1.00797																	2 He Helium 4.0026
3 Li Lithium 6.939	4 Be Beryllium 9.0122											5 B Boron 10.811	6 C Carbon 12.01115	7 N Nitrogen 14.0067	8 O Oxygen 15.9994	9 F Fluorine 18.9984	10 Ne Neon 20.183
11 Na Sodium 22.9898	12 Mg Magnesium 24.312											13 Al Aluminum 26.9815	14 Si Silicon 28.086	15 P Phosphorus 30.9738	16 S Sulfur 32.064	17 Cl Chlorine 35.453	18 Ar Argon 39.948
19 K Potassium 39.102	20 Ca Calcium 40.08	21 Sc Scandium 44.956	22 Ti Titanium 47.90	23 V Vanadium 50.942	24 Cr Chromium 51.996	25 Mn Manganese 54.9380	26 Fe Iron 55.847	27 Co Cobalt 58.9332	28 Ni Nickel 58.71	29 Cu Copper 63.54	30 Zn Zinc 65.37	31 Ga Gallium 69.72	32 Ge Germanium 72.59	33 As Arsenic 74.9216	34 Se Selenium 78.96	35 Br Bromine 79.909	36 Kr Krypton 83.80
37 Rb Rubidium 85.47	38 Sr Strontium 87.62	39 Y Yttrium 88.905	40 Zr Zirconium 91.22	41 Nb Niobium 92.906	42 Mo Molybdenum 95.94	43 Tc Technetium (99)	44 Ru Ruthenium 101.07	45 Rh Rhodium 102.905	46 Pd Palladium 106.4	47 Ag Silver 107.870	48 Cd Cadmium 112.40	49 In Indium 114.82	50 Sn Tin 118.69	51 Sb Antimony 121.75	52 Te Tellurium 127.60	53 I Iodine 126.9044	54 Xe Xenon 131.30
55 Cs Cesium 132.905	56 Ba Barium 137.34	57 La* Lanthanum 138.91	72 Hf Hafnium 178.49	73 Ta Tantalum 180.984	74 W (Tungsten) 183.85	75 Re Rhenium 186.2	76 Os Osmium 190.2	77 Ir Iridium 192.2	78 Pt Platinum 195.09	79 Au Gold 196.967	80 Hg Mercury 200.59	81 Tl Thallium 204.37	82 Pb Lead 207.19	83 Bi Bismuth 208.980	84 Po Polonium (210)	85 At Astatine (210)	86 Rn Radon (222)
87 Fr Francium (223)	88 Ra Radium (226)	89 Ac** Actinium (227)	105 Ha Hahnium (260)														
104 Ku Kurchatovium (260)																	

Lanthanide Series 6:

58 Ce Cerium 140.12	59 Pr Praseodymium 140.907	60 Nd Neodymium 144.24	61 Pm Promethium (147)	62 Sm Samarium 150.35	63 Eu Europium 151.96	64 Gd Gadolinium 157.25	65 Tb Terbium 158.924	66 Dy Dysprosium 162.50	67 Ho Holmium 164.9304	68 Er Erbium 167.26	69 Tm Thulium 168.934	70 Yb Ytterbium 173.04	71 Lu Lutetium 174.97

Actinide Series 7:

90 Th Thorium 232.038	91 Pa Protactinium (231)	92 U Uranium 238.03	93 Np Neptunium (237)	94 Pu Plutonium (242)	95 Am Americium (243)	96 Cm Curium (247)	97 Bk Berkelium (247)	98 Cf Californium (251)	99 Es Einsteinium (254)	100 Fm Fermium (253)	101 Md Mendelevium (256)	102 No Nobelium (254)	103 Lr Lawrencium (257)

The smallest and lightest atom is that of the element hydrogen. It has only 1 proton in its nucleus. Most hydrogen atoms have no neutrons, but a few have 1 neutron, and an even smaller number have 2 neutrons.

The biggest and heaviest atom found in nature is that of the element uranium. It has 92 protons in its nucleus. In most uranium nuclei (plural of *nucleus*), there are also 146 neutrons. The next most common number of neutrons found in uranium nuclei is 143.

Hydrogen is a light gas. Uranium is a very heavy solid. Hydrogen can combine with many different elements to form new substances. Only a few elements will join with uranium.

The differences between the elements depend on the number of protons. But atoms of the same element—with the same number of protons—can have fewer or more neutrons. Atoms with identical numbers of protons but with different numbers of neutrons are called **isotopes.**

All the various isotopes of an element are quite similar to each other. But they are not alike in mass. The more neutrons in an isotope, the greater the mass.

Every element has at least one isotope. But many elements have more than one.

Take hydrogen as an example. Hydrogen, we said, has 1 proton and no neutrons. But one isotope of hydrogen has 1

Hydrogen, the smallest and lightest element, is the chief component of the universe and makes up this cloud of stars, called a nebulosity.

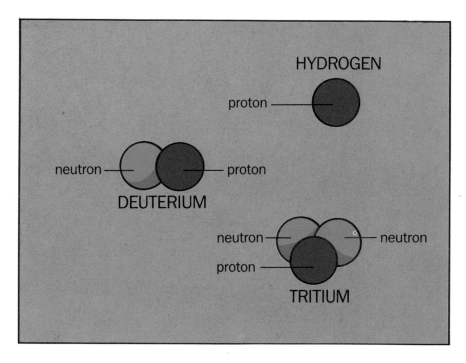

The nuclei of hydrogen and two of its isotopes.
The hydrogen nucleus is made up of one proton,
the deuterium nucleus is made up of one proton
and one neutron, and the tritium nucleus is made
up of one proton and two neutrons.

proton and 1 neutron. This isotope is called **deuterium.** Another hydrogen isotope has 1 proton and 2 neutrons. It is known as **tritium.**

Almost all uranium atoms found in nature are uranium-238. This means that they have 238 particles in their nuclei (92 protons and 146 neutrons). But an isotope of uranium, uranium-235, has 92 protons and 143 neutrons. In most ways, it is like uranium-238. But it is an isotope because of its three less neutrons.

In addition to the natural isotopes, there are also synthetic isotopes. These are created when scientists either add or remove neutrons from the nucleus of an atom. Many amazing advances in modern science have resulted from experiments with isotopes.

SOLIDS, LIQUIDS, AND GASES

All things are made of atoms. But not everything looks and feels the same. A chair, a drop of rain, a puff of air—they all look and feel very different.

Why?

They are different because of the way their atoms come together. In chairs—or rocks or books or pencils—the atoms are packed together in a particular order or arrangement. The chair, rock, book, and pencil are **solids**. Solids feel firm when you touch them. And they keep their shape.

Look around you. What other solids can you see or touch? All of these solids are made up of atoms pressed or crowded tightly together.

In some other things, such as water, milk, soda, and gasoline, the atoms are not packed together tightly and you can pour them. Substances that you can pour are **liquids**. When you touch most liquids, they feel soft and wet. Some liquids,

Above: perhaps there is nothing more solid-feeling than the earth we stand on. Yet the earth is composed of solids, liquids, and gases. *Center:* these folded, layered rocks are over 70 million years old. Rocks are often what we think of first when we think of solid matter, because of their firmness to the touch. *Below:* minerals are some of nature's most beautiful and colorful solids.

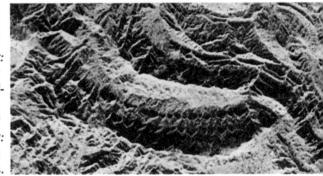

such as oil, just feel slippery. When you pour a liquid into a jar or bottle, the liquid takes on the shape of the container but does not expand to fill the space.

Here's a way to prove that there is space between the atoms in a liquid. Put exactly 1 cup of water into a measuring cup.

Now add a heaping tablespoon of salt to the water. Slowly stir it into the measuring cup. Now check the water level. Why didn't the level rise? Where did the salt go?

The water level did not rise because the salt went into the spaces between the atoms in the water. If there were no spaces there, the level would have gone up.

Water, milk, soda, and gasoline are liquids. Can you think of other kinds of liquids?

Finally, there are things in which the atoms are even more loosely packed than in liquids. Air, steam, and the helium used to blow up balloons are like that. Large spaces exist between their atoms. These things are called **gases.**

Adding salt to water, to prove that atoms have empty space

When you blow up a balloon, the gas inside spreads out and fills the available space.

You cannot see most gases. And unless they are moving—like a gust of wind—you cannot feel most gases. Gases do not have a shape of their own. Like liquids, they take on the shape of their container, but unlike liquids, they expand to fill all the space available by increasing their volume—that is, increasing the space between the atoms.

Suppose you blow air into a balloon. The air spreads out and fills the space. More than liquids, gases change not only their size and shape to fit the space available but their "size" (volume) as well.

You can squeeze lots of air into a small space. Then you have compressed air. Compressed air can have enough force to raise up an automobile!

The bubbles in soda contain one kind of gas. Another kind of gas is used in stoves for cooking or for heating the house. Do you know any other gases?

Some substances are found in all three states—solid, liquid, and gas. Take water, for example. Water is a liquid at room temperature and ordinary pressure. But when it becomes very cold it freezes and turns to ice, which is a solid. And when it becomes very hot it changes into steam, which is a gas.

Water in its three states

When water changes its state, it also changes the amount of space it fills. Get a clean, empty cottage cheese, yogurt, or margarine container. Fill it to the rim with water. Carefully set it in the freezer part of your refrigerator.

The next day, take out the container. Notice how the ice bulges up over the rim. This shows that the solid ice takes up more space than the liquid water. Now melt the ice and pour the water into a saucepan. Bring the water to a boil and notice the vapor go into the air. Water vapor is a gas. After a few minutes, pour the water from the saucepan back into the container. See how the water level is now below the rim?

Curiously enough, water is one of the few substances that increases in size when it freezes. Almost all other substances decrease in size. Bismuth, a metal, is an exception.

Everything in the universe is made of atoms. And all things are generally either solids, liquids, or gases. The difference is simply in the way the atoms are packed together.

MOLECULES
AND
COMPOUNDS

Atoms are joiners. They are almost always found in combination with other atoms. When two or more atoms join together they form a **molecule**. The elements are formed from molecules of identical atoms, for example, oxygen or nitrogen atoms.

Atoms of different elements also come together to form molecules. These are molecules of **compounds**. Just as atoms of the same kind make an element, so molecules of the same kind make a compound.

Water is a compound. Each molecule of water contains 2 hydrogen atoms and 1 oxygen atom. Another familiar compound is the salt that you sprinkle on food. Each molecule of salt contains 1 sodium atom and 1 chlorine atom.

Compounds can be a lot different from the elements they're made of. Here are some examples. Water is a liquid. Yet water is made up of the elements hydrogen and oxygen, which are both gases. Salt is a compound that is perfectly safe to eat.

Yet salt is made up of sodium and chlorine—both of which are poisons!

As we said earlier, there are only about a hundred different kinds of atoms or elements. But from these come thousands and thousands of different compounds.

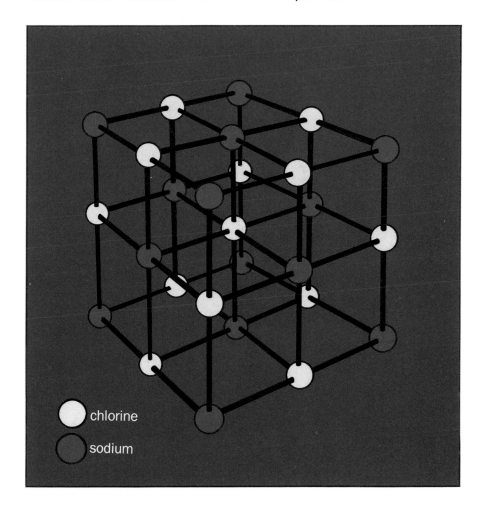

Molecules of the compound salt

You can compare atoms to letters of the alphabet. Just as there are only a hundred different kinds of atoms in the universe, so there are only twenty-six different letters in the alphabet. But think of how many words you can make with just those twenty-six letters! In the same way, the hundred different kinds of atoms can be made into more compounds than you can imagine.

Scientists have a quick way to show what atoms are in a compound. It is called a **chemical formula.** In the chemical formula for a compound, one or two letters stand for each element. The number after the element shows how many atoms of that element are in a single molecule of the compound.

We know that each molecule of water contains two atoms of hydrogen (H) and one atom of oxygen (O). The chemical formula for water, therefore, is H_2O.

Each molecule of salt contains one atom of sodium (Na) and one atom of chlorine (Cl). Its chemical formula is NaCl.

Both sugar and vinegar are compounds with more complex molecules. They both contain the same kinds of atoms, but in different numbers. Table sugar or sucrose has 12 carbon (C), 22 hydrogen (H), and 11 oxygen (O) atoms. Its formula is $C_{12}H_{22}O_{11}$. Vinegar has 2 carbon, 4 hydrogen, and 2 oxygen atoms. The chemical formula for vinegar is $C_2H_4O_2$.

Would you like to make a compound? Here's a way to make rust, which is a compound known as iron oxide. This form of iron oxide contains 2 atoms of iron (Fe) and 3 atoms of oxygen (O). The formula is Fe_2O_3.

For the iron, you'll need a piece of steel wool from the hardware or paint store, not a scouring pad from the grocery store that contains soap. Steel wool is made of iron. The oxygen will come from the air.

[30]

Making rust

Drop the steel wool into a glass jar. To speed up the joining of the iron and the oxygen, add a few drops of water to get the steel wool wet. Put a cover on the jar and set it aside.

Look at the steel wool at least once a day. In a short while, you'll see that it is changing. At first, it was a shiny gray color. Now it is becoming redder or browner. It is turning into rust. The change of color shows that the atoms of iron are combining with the atoms of oxygen in the air to form molecules of iron oxide.

Congratulations! You have brought together separate elements and created a compound.

ATOMS, ELECTRICITY, AND SUPERCONDUCTIVITY

You know that electricity lights up bulbs and runs machines. But do you know what electricity is?

Electricity is the flow of electrons from one atom to another.

Electrons are put to work making electricity in electric power plants. In these plants, huge magnets spin at high speed inside tightly wound loops of metal wire. Some of the electrons in the metal atoms are moving freely about from atom to atom. The spinning magnets—or coils of wire spinning near magnets—cause the electrons to move more easily in one direction than the other.

These fast-moving electrons bump into other electrons in nearby atoms. In the process, the electrons in these atoms are set free. The freed electrons fly off and strike electrons in other atoms. And so on. In a flash, a stream of electrons speeds down the entire length of the wire.

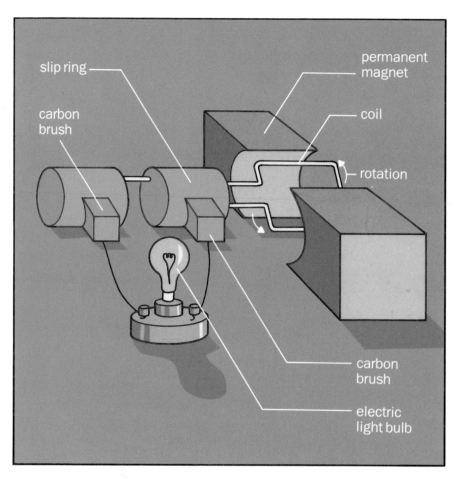

Magnetic coils spinning to create electricity

Actually, the electrons do not move all the way along the wire from the power plant to the electric light bulb. Instead, the electrons from the first atom knock loose the electrons in the second atom. These electrons head off for the third atom, while the first ones remain. The electrons from the second atom now strike the electrons in the third atom, leaving those from the second atom in their place, and so on. In this way, within a fraction of a second, the electricity reaches your lamp.

The flow of electrons can be compared to a row of falling dominoes. When you push the first domino, it knocks over the second. The second knocks over the third, which knocks over the fourth, all along the row. Each domino only moves enough to bump the next one. Like the dominoes, each electron only advances far enough to free up the next electron.

**Giant turbines at generating stations begin
the process of getting electricity to you.**

**Power lines take the electricity generated at
power plants and send it to homes and factories.**

The wire in the power plant is connected to long wires that run to houses, stores, factories, and all sorts of other buildings. Here the electricity is used to make light and heat. It is also used to run TV sets and refrigerators, stereos and electric clocks.

Just think of it. Electricity does so much work—and all as a result of electrons speeding through metal wires!

Because electricity flows quickly and easily through metal wires, we say that metal is a good **conductor** of electricity.

In general, the atoms of metals have just a few electrons in their outer shell. Therefore, it is easy for them to be knocked free by other electrons. When the outer shell has many electrons, it is much harder to loosen an electron.

But even metal wire is not a perfect conductor. It holds back, or stops, some of the flowing electricity. The wire *resists* the electrical flow.

Have you ever been part of a crowd that is trying to squeeze through a narrow doorway? The doorway offers resistance to the people passing through. In the same way, wire offers **resistance** to the flow of electricity.

Scientists have long known how to lower the resistance and increase the conductivity of wire. They have found that wire cooled down to nearly $-460°$ F $(-273°$ C$)$ loses all of its resistance. The electricity flows through without any loss. This is called **superconductivity.**

Superconductivity seemed to be of only limited usefulness, a laboratory curiosity, until quite recently. It could only be achieved by using very expensive liquid helium to cool the wires. But in 1985, scientists began finding ways to achieve superconductivity at higher temperatures and by using much less expensive liquid nitrogen.

Scientists are now able to achieve superconductivity with special ceramic materials instead of metal. One ceramic is made of the elements barium, yttrium, copper, and oxygen. It only needs to be cooled to $-281°$ F $(-174°$ C$)$ to become a superconductor.

The researchers studying superconductors think that they are on to something very exciting. They are experimenting with different combinations of elements. Sooner or later, they are quite sure that they will have a room temperature superconductor!

Reaching this goal will be a very important achievement. Resistance in the wires from the power plant will cause no

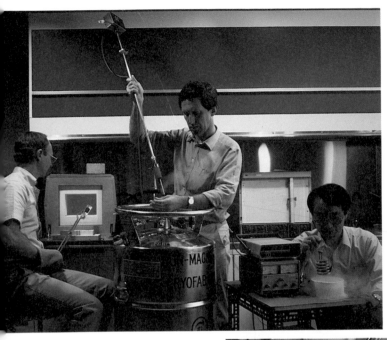

This picture shows the grinding and manufacturing (heating, cooling, and coating) of the newest superconductor ceramics.

In this picture we see the particle accelerator (atom smasher) at Fermi Lab near Chicago.

You can perhaps visualize how magnetic trains might someday travel along above the tracks by looking closely at this picture of a magnetic cylinder floating in air above a cylindrical piece of superconducting ceramic. The vapors are from the liquid nitrogen, which bathes the ceramic and keeps the temperatures low.

loss of electricity. Trains, powered by magnets, will travel along above the tracks at hundreds of miles an hour. Computers will become even smaller and faster. And there will be hundreds of other uses for superconductors that we can't even dream of today!

One of the uses for superconductors now being planned for the 1990s in the United States is the superconducting supercollider (SSC). This is a huge atom smasher, with an expected circumference of 100 miles (161 km). It will cost over $1 billion. With the SSC, atomic scientists will be able to do experiments (smashing atoms together) at much higher energy levels than ever before and thus learn much more about atoms and atomic particles.

RADIATION

For the most part, atomic nuclei stay the same. They do not gain or lose particles. Scientists say that atoms like this are "stable." Even when stable atoms join together to become a molecule, their nuclei do not change.

But from time to time, the nuclei of certain atoms do change. Parts of their nuclei come shooting out. These atoms are said to be **radioactive.**

There are a number of radioactive elements. The best known ones are radium, uranium, and radon. These elements go through a process called **radioactive decay.** They fling out tiny particles and bursts of energy from their nuclei.

In addition to the naturally occurring radioactive elements, a number of other elements can be made radioactive by adding or removing particles. These laboratory-made elements are called **radioactive isotopes.** They are said to be artificially radioactive.

The French scientists Marie and Pierre Curie.
Marie Curie is considered the discoverer of radiation.

One common method of creating radioactive isotopes is to bombard stable elements with neutrons. When a neutron strikes the nucleus of certain stable atoms, they become unstable and give off radiation.

Radioactive elements—natural or artificial—produce three types of radiation. They are named after the first three letters of the Greek alphabet—alpha, beta, and gamma.

Alpha radiation is actually made up of particles. Each alpha particle consists of 2 protons and 2 neutrons. These particular four particles also make up the helium atom, but with its 2 electrons stripped away. Put another way, the alpha particle is the nucleus of the helium atom. Since the protons have a positive charge and the neutrons have no charge at all, the alpha particle is positively charged.

Beta radiation also consists of particles. But study has shown that the beta particles are the same as electrons! Electrons, as you know, have very little mass and carry a negative charge.

Gamma radiation is more a ray of high energy than a particle. It is like an X-ray. Gamma rays have no electrical charge. They are neutral.

As radioactive elements decay, the radiation is released from the nuclei of the atoms. This leads to changes in the number and types of particles. As a result, the element itself becomes a different element. In time, most of the natural radioactive elements become lead, which has a stable nucleus. Once the nucleus is stable, the radioactive decay stops.

Scientists measure some types of radioactivity with a Geiger counter, which counts the number of particles or rays that strike its surface. The more strikes, the higher the level of radiation. Photographic film is also a radiation detector.

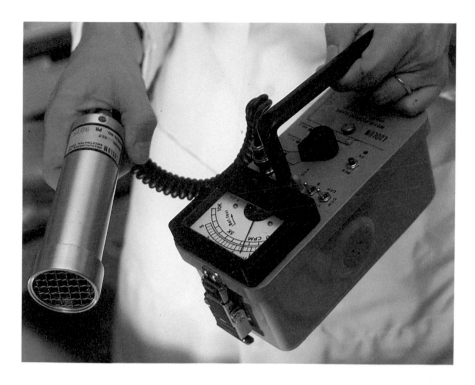

A Geiger counter is used to detect radioactivity.

Another measure of radioactivity is **half-life**. The half-life is the time it takes for half of the atoms of a radioactive element to decay.

The half-life of some highly unstable radioactive isotopes is just a tiny fraction of a second. One isotope of radon, a radioactive gas, has a half-life of slightly less than four days. The element radium, which is produced from uranium decay, has a half-life of 1,600 years. The half-life of uranium is 4.5 billion years. And thorium, a radioactive element present in certain minerals, has a half-life of 14 billion years!

The radiation given off by radioactive elements is dangerous to humans and other living things. Most living beings struck by a large amount of radiation suffer severe damage or death. The radiation can cause burns, rashes, hair loss, or other symptoms to occur immediately. Sometimes, though, the cells may be damaged in ways that are not noticeable at first. But over many years, the changes can lead to cancer.

Someday, you may see a bright yellow-and-black radiation warning sign on a door, building, or large metal drum. Take care not to get too close. The radiation that you cannot see, feel, or smell can cause you terrible harm.

Never get too close when you see this warning sign.

EXPLODING ATOMS

Back in the Middle Ages, alchemists, people who combined chemistry and magic, tried to find a way to change lead into silver or gold. None ever succeeded in changing one element into another. But in 1939, some scientists found that if they bombarded uranium with neutrons, they created two other elements—barium and krypton—plus a few more neutrons!

They knew that there are 92 protons in the uranium nucleus. This is the sum of the protons in barium (56) and krypton (36): 56 + 36 = 92. They concluded that the entering neutrons split the nucleus of the uranium atoms in two, producing barium and krypton. Splitting an atom became known as **nuclear fission.**

Scientists soon learned two things about nuclear fission. One, of course, was that the uranium atom split into barium and krypton. Two, there was a tremendous release of energy at the same time. But the big question was: Where did this energy come from?

[45]

The answer came from Albert Einstein's special theory of relativity. Einstein showed that a small amount of mass can become a fantastic amount of energy. His famous equation, $E = mc^2$, tells the story. The energy (E) in matter is equal to its mass (m) times the speed of light (186,000 miles, or 300,000 km, per second) multiplied by itself (c^2), that is, squared.

In nuclear fission, the mass of the barium, krypton, and the extra neutrons together is slightly less than the mass of the uranium. It is this lost mass that produces the burst of energy. But nuclear fission does not stop after a single uranium atom is split. The split atom also releases more neutrons. These neutrons then fly out and split other uranium atoms. Thus the fission keeps going. The process is called a **chain reaction.**

A very fast chain reaction produces a huge explosion. This is the basic idea behind the atom bomb. But there are ways to slow down the chain reaction. Rods of the element cadmium or boron can be placed in with the uranium. The cadmium or boron captures some of the flying neutrons. With fewer neutrons, fewer uranium atoms are split. This slows down the chain reaction.

Nuclear reactors are devices that slow down and control the chain reaction of nuclear fission. Instead of causing a powerful explosion, the reactors produce heat. This heat can then be used just like the heat from burning oil or coal. Nuclear reactors are used to produce electricity in power stations and to run the engines of nuclear submarines.

Much more heat comes from splitting atoms than from burning oil or coal. Splitting the atoms in just 1 pound (0.45 kg) of uranium gives off as much heat as burning 3 million pounds (1.4 million kg) of coal!

[46]

Top: an early atomic explosion at a Nevada test site. *Inset:* nuclear fuel rods, used to slow down a chain reaction. *Bottom:* the core of a nuclear reactor, where the fission takes place.

But nuclear reactors are a mixed blessing. They make lots of heat. But they also produce dangerous—even deadly—radiation. Reactors are usually surrounded with thick lead and concrete shielding. This is to protect the workers at the reactor and the public for miles around. Still, many people fear accidents that can release the radiation and cause sickness or death for thousands of people.

Reactors are surrounded by thick cement and lead shields, and are usually near a source of water for emergency cooling of the core and radioactive waste.

The experimental Tokamak Fusion Test Reactor at Princeton plasma physics laboratory. Here, scientists are trying to learn how to create electricity from the joining, rather than the splitting, of atoms.

In the early 1950s, scientists found a new way to release energy from inside the nucleus of the atom. Instead of splitting large atoms such as uranium, they combined the nuclei of small atoms, like hydrogen. This is called **nuclear fusion.**

Nuclear fusion is always going on in the sun and other stars. It produces the light and heat that comes to earth from the sun. The first human attempt at nuclear fusion was the superpowerful hydrogen, or thermonuclear, bomb.

Ordinary hydrogen atoms alone (1 proton, no neutrons) cannot be used for nuclear fusion. The hydrogen bomb works with the two heavier isotopes of hydrogen—deuterium (1 proton, 1 neutron) and tritium (1 proton, 2 neutrons). When the nuclei of these isotopes combine, or fuse, they produce helium (2 protons, 2 neutrons). At the same time, the fusion releases the extra neutron and a gigantic burst of energy.

We have had the hydrogen bomb for a long time. Yet scientists are still not able to build a nuclear fusion reactor for peaceful uses. There are two basic problems: How do you produce the extremely hot (in the millions of degrees) temperatures needed to bring the hydrogen nuclei together? And then, how do you build a container strong enough to hold the superhot hydrogen gas?

Researchers are now trying some new approaches. Very strong magnetic fields and powerful laser beams are being used to heat the hydrogen and hold it while the nuclear fusion occurs.

The future looks very bright. By the end of the century, nuclear fusion may be available as a cheap, clean, relatively safe, and efficient source of energy.

THE
PARTICLE ZOO

In the year 1900, scientists believed that atoms consisted of three particles—electrons, protons, and neutrons. Since then, many more so-called subatomic particles have been found. Scientists now know about two hundred such particles! The many new and strange particles have come to be called the **particle zoo.**

Of the many "wild beasts" in the particle zoo, probably four are best known. They are the **positron, neutrino, photon,** and **meson.**

The positrons were discovered accidentally in **cosmic rays** in 1932, although scientists predicted their existence before that. Cosmic rays are streams of high-energy particles that strike earth from space. Among the many particles was one that was particularly strange. It had the same mass as an electron. But it did not have the negative electrical charge of an ordinary electron. This particle had a *positive* electrical charge! Hence, it was given the name *positron*, short for "positive electron."

One fact about the positron is particularly amazing. As soon as it collides with an electron, the two particles destroy each other. The positron and electron both disappear. All that is left is a burst of energy!

The positron is an example of an **antiparticle.** It has the same mass and the same amount of charge as the electron— but of the opposite charge. Soon researchers found that every particle has its own antiparticle. And whenever a particle and an antiparticle meet, both instantly vanish with a release of energy.

Scientists can calculate exactly how much energy is released in radioactive decay. But studies showed that less energy was emitted during radioactive decay than they expected.

What happened to the missing energy? In 1930, the Austrian-American physicist Wolfgang Pauli suggested that there was another particle, which had not yet been observed, that carried the missing energy away. Other scientists stated that such a particle had no mass and no electrical charge. This particle came to be called a neutrino.

But then, after describing and naming the particle, the scientists were faced with a problem. No one could find a neutrino! Neutrinos are very hard to find because they hardly ever interact with other matter. One atomic scientist predicted that a neutrino would have to pass through a solid block of lead 21 billion billion miles thick before it would interact with another particle! Yet, in 1953, two American physicists, Clyde Cowan and Frederick Reines, were able to prove that neutrinos do exist.

Neutrino detectors, such as this one, were originally built to look for proton decay. Proton decay has never been proven. By using these devices, scientists can plot the activity of neutrinos, especially when there has been a large burst of them, such as from an exploding star. Inset: Wolfgang Pauli, the scientist who first suggested the existence of the neutrino.

Negative and positive electrical charges attract each other. This is a well-known fact. But what is the cause of the force that draws positive and negative particles together?

Scientists discovered that a particle, called a photon, carries the electric force. Photons are particles of light energy. They have no mass and no electrical charge. And they always travel at the speed of light (186,000 miles, or 300,000 km, per second). It is the photon's electric force that holds the negative electrons in their shells around the atom's positive nucleus.

One expert compares the inside of a hydrogen atom to a tennis game. The game has two players, the proton in the nucleus and the electron in orbit. They keep on hitting the ball—the photon—back and forth from one to the other.

Another important question about atoms had to be answered: What holds the protons and neutrons together in the nucleus? Scientists knew it had to be a very strong force. The protons in the nucleus all have a positive electrical charge. Since particles of like charges push each other away, or repel each other, the nucleus should fly apart. Yet something keeps it together.

Experts looked for a particle that acted as the "glue" inside the nucleus. The particle's mass, they guessed, was about halfway between that of the electron and the proton. So they called it *mesotron,* from the Greek word for "middle." Later the name was shortened to meson.

Two kinds of mesons were eventually found. One was called pi-meson, which was shortened to **pion.** The other, mu-meson, became **muon.**

The pion carries the strong force in the nucleus. Pions have 270 times the mass of the electron. They may have positive or negative charges or be neutral. And they have an average lifespan of about one hundred-millionth of a second. The muon is more closely related to the electron. It is not now considered a meson.

The particle zoo does indeed have some very strange creatures!

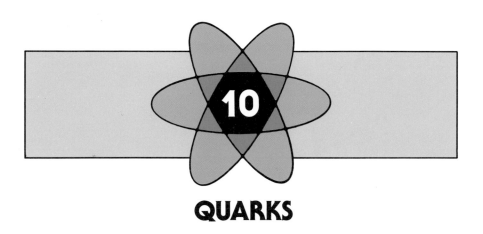

QUARKS

Scientists believe that about 15 billion years ago—give or take 5 billion years—our entire universe was crushed and squeezed into a tiny bit of superhot, superheavy matter. Then, in what is now called the **Big Bang,** this little speck exploded in a colossal burst of energy and particles.

The particles that were flung out in the Big Bang were not atoms. They were not even atomic particles such as protons, neutrons, or electrons. Nor were they any of the two hundred or so inmates of the "particle zoo." They were what we now consider the most basic, most fundamental building blocks of all matter. The modern name for these prime particles is **quarks.** (Quarks rhymes with *corks,* not with *sparks.*) Starting right after the Big Bang, the quarks began coming together to form the particles that we know today.

Although quarks are billions of years old, it took scientists until the 1960s to become aware of their existence. The

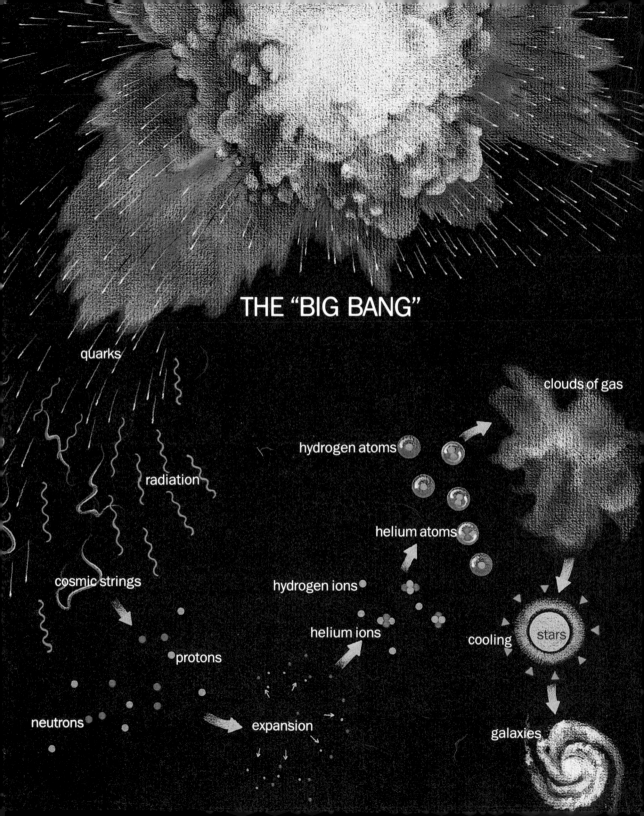

THE "BIG BANG"

quarks

clouds of gas

hydrogen atoms

radiation

helium atoms

cosmic strings

hydrogen ions

protons

helium ions

cooling · stars

neutrons

expansion

galaxies

leading figure in this important discovery was the American physicist, Murray Gell-Mann. It was Gell-Mann who first suggested that the proton, neutron, meson, and some other particles are actually made up of quarks. Just as banana, ice cream, hot fudge, and whipped cream go together to make a banana split, so different kinds of quarks combine to make these subatomic particles.

No scientist has ever seen or touched an isolated quark. There is no proof that quarks exist. But right now quarks are the best way of explaining the way atoms behave. That is why almost everyone believes in these particles within particles.

According to Gell-Mann's theory, there are three types of quarks. They differ in their mass and electrical charge. Playfully, he called this difference the **flavors** of quarks. He named the three flavors **up, down,** and **sideways.** Later, sideways was changed to **strange.**

These flavors have nothing to do with food flavors, such as chocolate or vanilla. Flavors are only a fanciful way to describe the different quarks.

In time, researchers had some new thoughts about quarks. Not all quarks of the same flavor are alike. Each flavor comes in three types. These types are known as **colors.** The colors refer to the different ways the quarks join with other quarks. They are not at all related to the actual color of the quarks.

Scientists use the names of different colors to describe quarks. Red, blue, and green are the most popular.

Once they began using color names, the scientists worked out what they call the **color rule.** According to the rule, a particle that contains three quarks must have one of each color.

In the 1970s, two more flavors were found beyond the original three flavors. One flavor is **charm.** The other is called either **bottom** or **beauty.**

Then, in the 1980s, another idea was introduced. Quark flavors come in pairs, scientists said. Up and down made one pair. Strange and charm made another. And there had to be one more. It was named either **top** to go with bottom or **truth** to go with beauty.

And that is where matters stand today. We know of eighteen quarks. There are the six flavors—up and down, strange and charm, truth and beauty. And each flavor comes in three colors—red, blue, and green.

Up Red	Up Blue	Up Green
Down Red	Down Blue	Down Green
Strange Red	Strange Blue	Strange Green
Charm Red	Charm Blue	Charm Green
Truth Red	Truth Blue	Truth Green
Beauty Red	Beauty Blue	Beauty Green

What about the future? Will scientists find more particles within the atom? Will they find a more basic particle to replace the quark as the building block of all matter?

No one can answer these questions today. But you can be sure that brilliant minds are at work in labs all over the world trying to learn more about our atomic world!

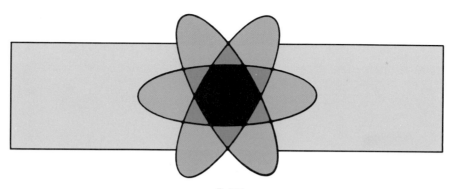

AN
ATOMIC
DICTIONARY

The following terms, highlighted in bold-faced letters in the text, form the basic vocabulary used by chemists, atomic physicists, cosmologists, and other scientists in formulating new theories and developing ideas.

antiparticle. A subatomic particle with the same mass as another particle but the opposite electrical charge.

atom. The smallest possible unit of a substance.

Big Bang. The enormous explosion thought by most scientists today to have created the universe, some 15 billion years ago.

chain reaction. The process that occurs when an atom is split in nuclear fission, causing the release of energy and a neutron from the nucleus of an atom, which strikes another atom and releases more energy and another neutron, etc.

colors. A kind of designation for various flavors of one kind of quark.

compound. A substance made up of molecules of different kinds of elements.

conductor. A metal or other material that allows electricity to flow freely through it.

cosmic rays. Streams of high-energy particles that strike the earth from space.

electricity. The flow of electrons from one atom to another along a wire.

electron. A negatively charged subatomic particle that revolves around the nucleus of an atom.

element. A substance made up of molecules of only one kind of atom, such as oxygen, which contains only oxygen atoms.

flavors. Types of quarks. There are now three known flavors—*up, down,* and *strange.*

gas. A substance that expands to fill the available space and takes on the shape of its container.

isotopes. Variations of the same element. The difference lies in the number of neutrons in the nuclei of the atoms.

liquid. A substance that can be poured and that usually feels soft and wet.

meson. A subatomic particle with a mass about halfway between that of an electron and a proton. The meson is considered the "glue" inside the nucleus, holding the nucleus together.

molecule. A chain of atoms of an element or a compound. Molecules within elements are made up of like atoms. Molecules of compounds are made up of different atoms.

muon. A subatomic particle once considered a kind of meson, now thought to more closely resemble the electron.

neutrino. A subatomic particle with little or no mass and no electrical charge.

neutron. A subatomic particle found in the nucleus of an atom; contains no charge.

nuclear fission. The splitting of an atom, to release subatomic particles and energy from the nucleus. Used for energy generation and atomic weapons.

nuclear fusion. The fusing together, or joining, of the nuclei of atoms, which results in energy being given off that can then be used to generate electricity. The sun uses nuclear fusion to produce its heat and light.

nucleus. The central core of the atom, containing the protons and any neutrons.

photon. A particle of light energy with no mass and no electrical charge.

pion. A kind of meson, carrying the so-called strong force in the nucleus.

positron. A subatomic particle with the same mass as an electron but with a positive electrical charge.

proton. The positively charged subatomic particle in the nucleus of an atom.

quarks. The most fundamental building blocks of all matter. Quarks make up some of the subatomic particles and in the early universe probably existed in a free state.

radioactive decay. The process by which certain unstable elements, such as uranium, emit particles and energy from their nuclei. Eventually the element changes into another element.

solid. A substance that feels firm to the touch and keeps its shape.

superconductivity. The flow of electricity through a kind of conductor that has no resistance at all.

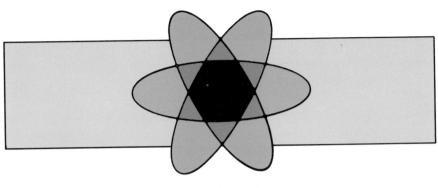

INDEX